What Can You Do with an
Old Red Shoe?

A Green Activity Book About Reuse

Anna Alter

Christy Ottaviano Books
Henry Holt and Company
New York

For my very supportive friends

Henry Holt and Company, LLC
Publishers since 1866
175 Fifth Avenue
New York, New York 10010
www.HenryHoltKids.com

Henry Holt® is a registered trademark of Henry Holt and Company, LLC.
Copyright © 2009 by Anna Alter
All rights reserved.

Distributed in Canada by H. B. Fenn and Company Ltd.

Library of Congress Cataloging-in-Publication Data
Alter, Anna.
What can you do with an old red shoe? :
a green activity book about re-use / Anna Alter. — 1st ed.
p.   cm. — (Christy Ottaviano books)
ISBN-13: 978-0-8050-8290-6
ISBN-10: 0-8050-8290-5
1. Handicraft—Juvenile literature. 2. Waste products—Juvenile literature.
3. Recycling (Waste, etc.)—Juvenile literature. 4. Salvage (Waste, etc.)—Juvenile literature. I. Title.
TT157.A46 2009 745.5—dc22 2008018341

First Edition—2009
Designed by Elynn Cohen
The artist used acrylic paints on BFK Rives printmaking paper
to create the illustrations for this book.
Printed in China on acid-free paper. ∞

1 3 5 7 9 10 8 6 4 2

Introduction

This book is all about the ways in which you can reuse and recycle. Each project introduces an art activity that reuses materials you can find in your home. Some of the activities require the help of an adult.

Reusing is a fun way to reinvent worn items. It's also a great way to help conserve our natural resources (like the trees used to make paper) and create less trash to store in landfills. By finding new ways to use old things instead of throwing them away, we can help to keep the environment clean and healthy. If we share in the responsibility of taking care of our world, we can all enjoy it together!

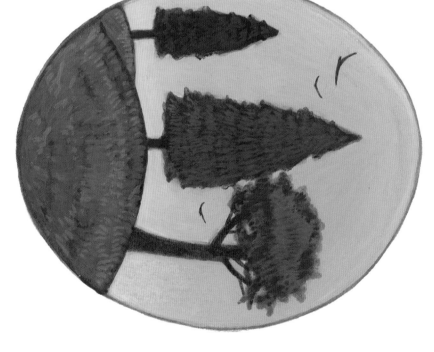

Contents

Activities that require adult assistance

The waves came in creeping,
stealing, and sweeping—
they snatched Sarah's flip-flop,
and took it away!

The shoe went afloat,
like a pink plastic boat,
and some lazy old crab
had a ship for a day!

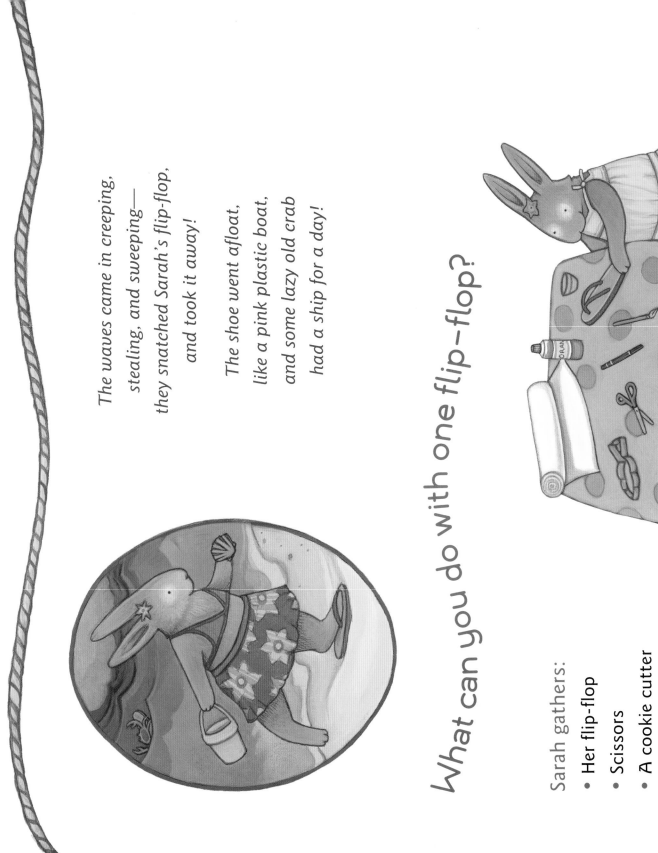

What can you do with one flip-flop?

Sarah gathers:

- Her flip-flop
- Scissors
- A cookie cutter
- A marker
- A paintbrush
- Paint and a dish
- Paper

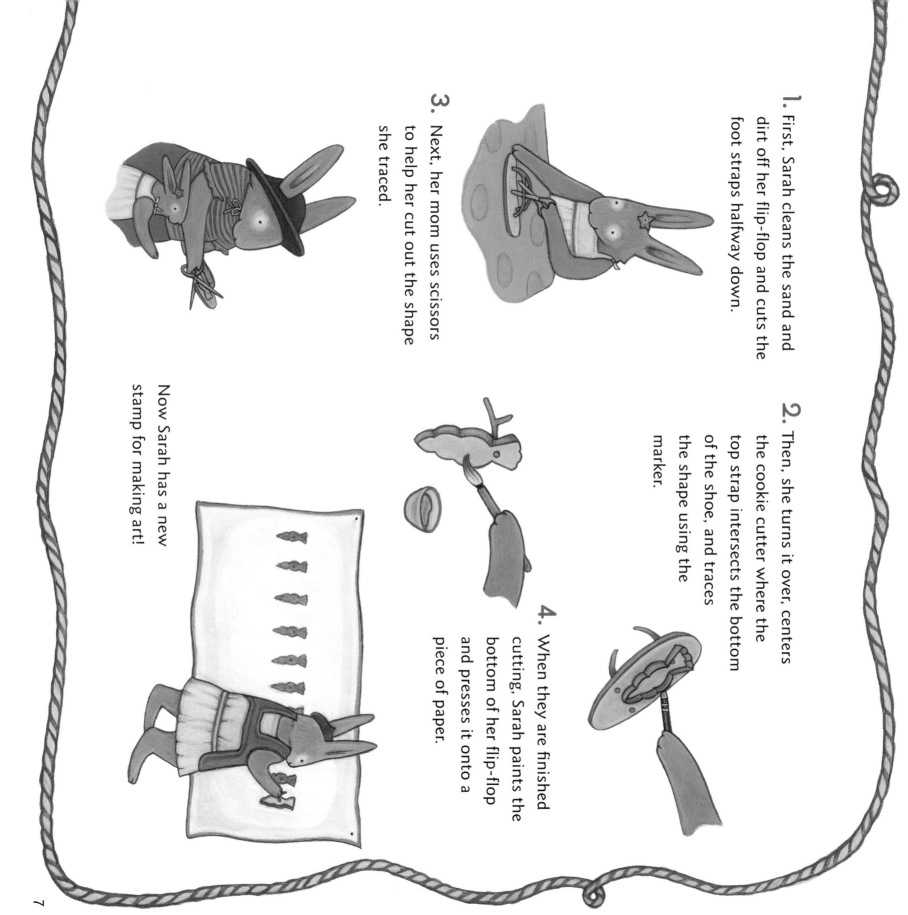

1. First, Sarah cleans the sand and dirt off her flip-flop and cuts the foot straps halfway down.

2. Then, she turns it over, centers the cookie cutter where the top strap intersects the bottom of the shoe, and traces the shape using the marker.

3. Next, her mom uses scissors to help her cut out the shape she traced.

4. When they are finished cutting, Sarah paints the bottom of her flip-flop and presses it onto a piece of paper.

Now Sarah has a new stamp for making art!

Ben wore his bulldozer T-shirt all week. . . .

On Monday, he spilled chocolate milk down the front.

On Tuesday, it caught in his locker.

On Wednesday, a thread got stuck in his desk.

On Thursday, it ripped during soccer.

On Friday, he fell in a puddle three times.

By Saturday, it was all covered in dirt.

So Sunday, his mom took it out of the closet

and gave him a tractor T-shirt.

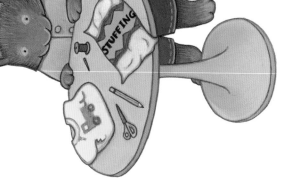

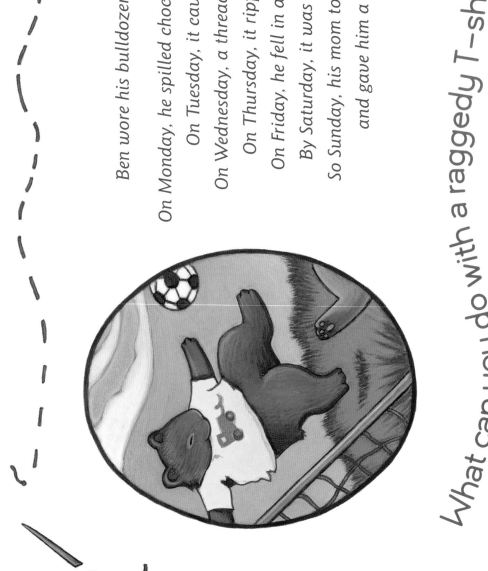

What can you do with a raggedy T-shirt?

Ben gathers:

- An old T-shirt (washed)
- A pencil
- Scissors
- A needle and thread
- Pillow stuffing

1. First, Ben draws a rectangle on the chest of his shirt with a pencil. (He could also draw a circle or triangle shape.)

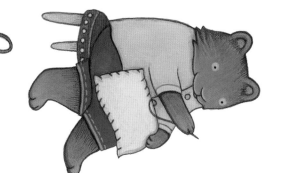

2. Then, he cuts along his outline, making sure to cut through both the front and back of the shirt.

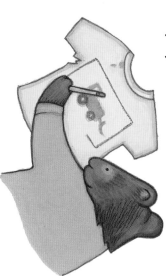

3. Next, he flips over the pieces he's cut so that the bulldozer design is on the inside. He sews around the edges with his needle and thread, leaving about five inches of fabric unsewn. (His dad could help sew the seam if Ben needs him to.)

Now his favorite T-shirt is his favorite pillow!

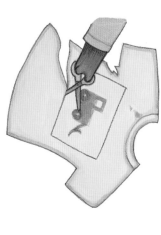

4. Ben turns the pillow right side out and stuffs it with pillow stuffing. When the pillow is stuffed, he sews up the hole with his needle and thread.

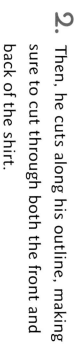

Fred was taking a shower this morning,
when something crashed on his head.
The curtain that hung on the side of the shower
had ripped down,
then dropped down,
then came down on Fred!

What can you do with a ripped shower curtain?

Fred gathers:

- An old plastic shower curtain
- A measuring tape
- A crayon
- Scissors
- A needle and heavyweight thread

1. First, Fred measures the distance from the top of his chest to his knees.

2. Then, he draws and cuts five shapes out of his curtain:

a square with each side as long as the distance he just measured . . .

and four strips as long as his measurement and one-inch wide.

3. Fred draws a small square in the top two corners of the large square, then cuts along the lines.

4. Fred sews one curtain strip to each of the top two corners of the large piece with his needle and thread. (If the plastic is too thick to sew, Fred will ask his mom for help.)

5. Next, he sews the remaining two strips to the sides of the main piece.

Now Fred has an apron to wear when he makes art!

When Ruby puts on her red dancing shoes,
she can't wait to strut down the street.
She never needs music to tango round town—
she goes by the beat of her feet.

After whirling a waltz up seventeen blocks,
Ruby wore out her shoes in the toe.
Still she curtsied and bowed to the gathering crowd,
a dancing queen out on the go.

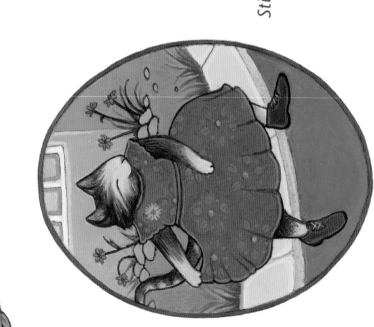

What can you do with an old red shoe?

Ruby gathers:

- Her old red shoe
- A dust rag
- A measuring tape
- A small flower pot
- A starter plant (Ruby chooses pansies)
- Potting soil

1. First, Ruby cleans off her shoe with the dust rag, especially the sole.

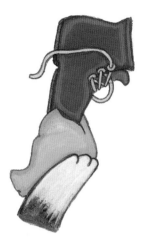

2. Next, she measures around the opening at the top of the shoe.

3. Then, Ruby uses that measurement to choose a pot that is just a little bit smaller. She plants some pansies inside it, surrounding the roots with soil.

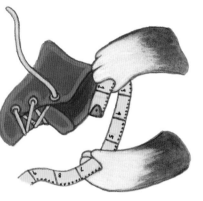

4. She places the potted plant in her shoe and pulls the laces tight, tying them at the top, so that the pot is held securely.

Now Ruby has a planter that reminds her of all the fun she had in her favorite shoes!

Jack's blanket was stained,
it was damp,
it was done—
a mere ghost of a blanket
made pale from the sun.
The fabric had worn,
a soft gauze to the touch.
Jack gave it a squeeze
for he loved it so much.

What can you do with a worn blanket?

Jack gathers:

- His worn blanket
- A ruler
- A pencil or marker
- Scissors
- A needle and thread

To do another project, he also gathers:

- An old pair of jeans

1. First, Jack draws an eight-inch square on the blanket.

2. Then, he carefully cuts out the square he has drawn.

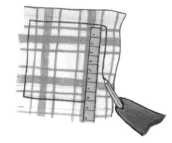

3. He finishes the edges by folding over half an inch of the fabric and sewing it in place. (His dad helps with the sewing.)

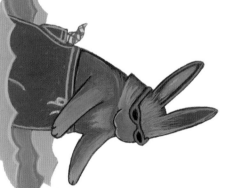

Now he takes his new handkerchief with him every-where, even to the pool!

What can Jack do with the rest of his blanket?

1. First, Jack cuts out a piece of his blanket that overlaps a hole in his jeans by one inch. (He can use a ruler to measure, or place the blanket under the hole and trace its shape.)

2. Next, he places the piece over the hole. Jack's dad helps him to fold under the edge of the fabric by about half an inch, pin it in place, then sew it down with a sewing machine.

Now his old jeans are patched, and they match his new handkerchief!

15

The sun beamed down on the strawberry patch.
Gertrude beamed down on the pile of berries
that sat on her lap
as she sat in the dirt,
one hand in the basket that sat on her skirt.

The sun hung low on the strawberry patch.
Gertrude looked down at her empty green basket.
She wiped off her chin,
her belly was fed,
then took off for home with her fingers dyed red.

What can you do with empty berry baskets?

Gertrude gathers:

- 3 empty berry baskets (cleaned)
- A long strip of cardboard that is as wide
  as one berry basket
- A pencil
- Scissors
- String, twine, or yarn
- Decorative ribbon scraps
- Markers

1. First, Gertrude lines up the berry baskets on her cardboard. She uses a pencil to mark four spots where there are holes at the bottom of each basket.

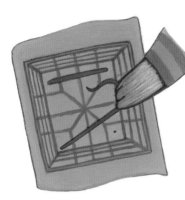

2. Next, she removes the baskets and asks her dad to use scissors to punch holes where the pencil marks are.

3. Gertrude puts a basket back on the cardboard. She threads a piece of yarn or string up through a hole in the cardboard, over the bottom of the basket, then back down through another hole, continuing until the basket is laced on the board. When both ends of the string are on the bottom of the cardboard, she ties them together. She does the same for the other two baskets.

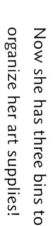

4. Gertrude decorates her baskets by weaving ribbon and yarn scraps in and out around the holes in the basket, then ties together the loose ends. She writes the names of the art supplies she plans to store in front of each basket on the cardboard.

Now she has three bins to organize her art supplies!

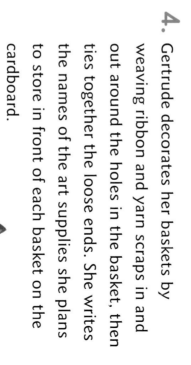

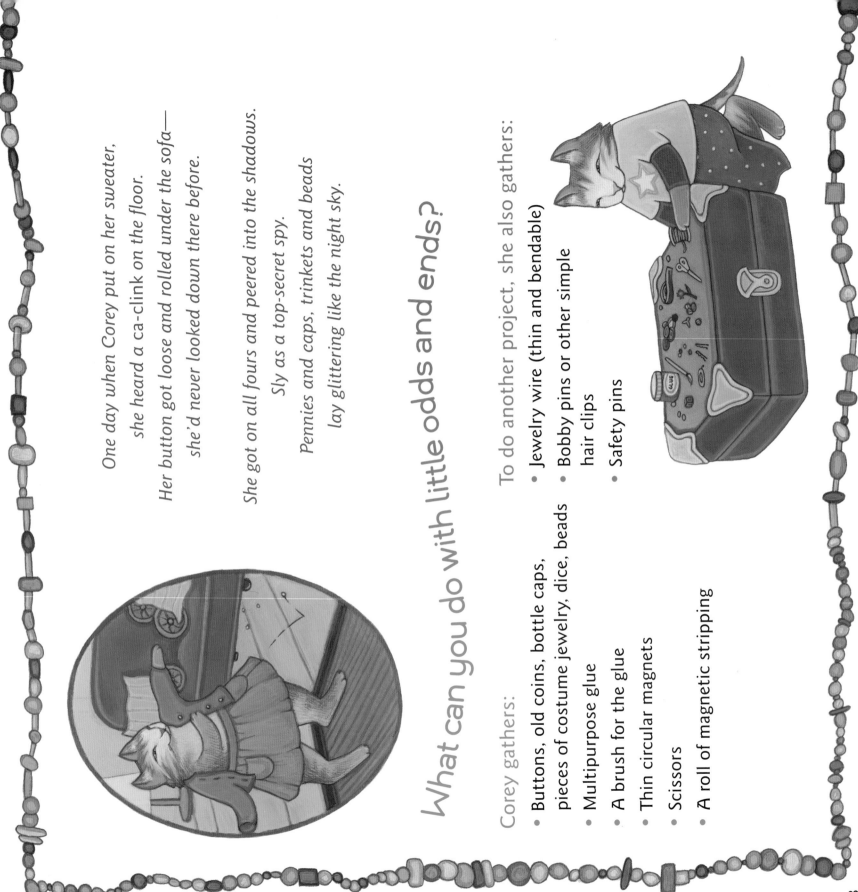

One day when Corey put on her sweater,
she heard a ca-clink on the floor.
Her button got loose and rolled under the sofa—
she'd never looked down there before.

She got on all fours and peered into the shadows.
Sly as a top-secret spy.
Pennies and caps, trinkets and beads
lay glittering like the night sky.

What can you do with little odds and ends?

Corey gathers:

- Buttons, old coins, bottle caps, pieces of costume jewelry, dice, beads
- Multipurpose glue
- A brush for the glue
- Thin circular magnets
- Scissors
- A roll of magnetic stripping

To do another project, she also gathers:

- Jewelry wire (thin and bendable)
- Bobby pins or other simple hair clips
- Safety pins

1. Corey uses glue to stick her odds and ends onto magnets. Sometimes she glues these treasures onto circular magnets, and sometimes she uses strips of magnet cut from her roll.

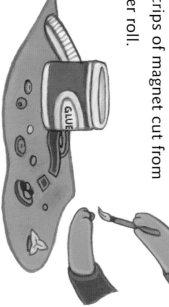

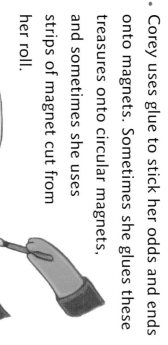

Now she has fun magnets to use to decorate the refrigerator, her locker, or even her mailbox!

What can Corey do with the rest of her odds and ends?

1. Corey separates out odds and ends that have a hole, such as beads, buttons, or jewelry pieces.

2. Then she takes jewelry wire and ties them to her bobby pins, barrettes, or safety pins. If she wants to make a barrette with the odds and ends that don't have holes, then she uses glue.

Now Corey has lots of beautiful new jewelry to wear, and she didn't even have to go to the store!

Peter loves canned soup to eat.
Without a spoon, he's not complete.
He keeps a can in his backseat.
He'll even try red soup with beets.

The cupboard's full of tin-can stacks
in case he needs a late-night snack.
They just might reach the polar caps,
if they were piled back-to-back!

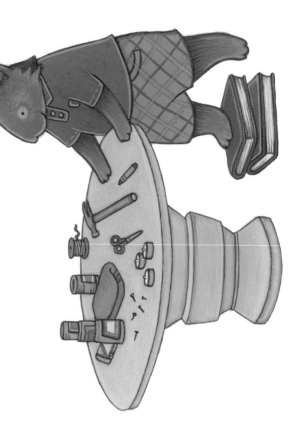

What can you do with empty tin cans?

Peter gathers:

- An empty tin can*
  (lid removed by an adult)
- A crayon
- Small towel
- A hammer
- Nails (sharp)
- Scissors
- Thin wire
- Tea light candle

* Thinner cans are easier to puncture.

1. First, Peter takes his can and peels off the label. (It helps to first soak it in water.)

2. Next, he uses a crayon to draw a star (or another simple shape) onto his can.

3. Peter lets his mom help him with the next step. First, she folds a small towel and puts the can on top so it doesn't roll. Then, she uses a hammer and nails to punch holes along the lines of the star, about three eighths of an inch apart.**

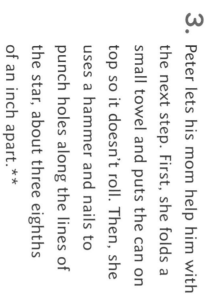

4. Last, she punches two holes across from each other at the top edge of the can. Peter strings wire through and places a candle inside for his mother to light.

Now Peter has a glowing lantern to admire when the sun goes down!

** If the can dents when nails go in, try filling it with water and putting it in the freezer until the water freezes solid before making holes.

Trina is an artist
who doesn't like to stop.
She's colored the walls in her art room,
the bottom to the top.

The walls are one big canvas
and never look complete.
She's worn out all her crayons—
a great artistic feat.

What can you do with bits of old crayon?

Trina gathers:

- Lots of used crayons
- An old metal bowl or pot
(used only for crafts)
- An ice cube tray

1. First, Trina removes the paper wrappers from her crayons.

2. Next, she puts them in her metal bowl, one color at a time. Then she asks her dad to heat the oven to 250 degrees and put the bowl inside for 10 minutes.

3. When the crayons have melted, Trina's dad helps her pour the colored wax into an ice cube tray.*

4. Trina puts the tray into the refrigerator so that the cubes will cool. This will take about 30 minutes.

5. When the crayons have cooled, Trina turns over the tray on the counter, and out come her newly formed crayon cubes.

Now Trina can start drawing all over again!

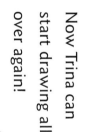

* If Trina wants to make multicolored cubes, first, she melts one crayon color and pours it into the ice cube tray. Then, when it has cooled slightly, she adds another color.

When December rolls around,
and the blue sky has faded to gray,
the snow makes our city a playground,
so we run to the hilltop to play.

Jon turns to the calendar's very last page
and counts down to the thirty-first day.
He's flipped over June, October, and March,
August, September, and May.

What can you do with an old calendar?

Jon gathers:

- An old paper calendar
- Scissors
- Velcro dots
- A ruler
- Poster board
- Markers

1. First, Jon takes his old calendar and cuts out the calendar squares from a month with thirty-one days.

2. Then, he flips them over and sticks the soft side of the Velcro dots to the back of the squares.

FRONT   BACK

←

3. Next, he uses his ruler to draw a grid on the bottom half of a piece of poster board that is seven squares wide by six squares tall. Above them, he draws a rectangle.

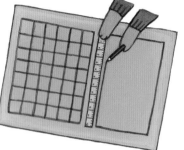

4. Jon writes the days of the week above each column of squares, then decorates the rest of the poster board with markers.

5. He sticks the rough side of the Velcro dots to the middle of each square on the poster board and one to each corner of the large rectangle.

Each month Jon draws a new picture to Velcro to the top half of his reusable calendar!

6. When he is ready to put the numbers on his calendar, he checks his computer to find out which number of the month falls on which day.

When the holidays are over,
there's crinkly paper torn and crunched,
tissue paper wrinkled wrongly,
cards and ribbons in a bunch.

Angelina puts her presents
back in boxes as before,
wrinkly wrappings loosely round,
so she can open them once more!

What can you do with used wrapping paper?

Angelina gathers:

- Used gift wrappings (including tissue paper and cards)
- Scissors
- Construction paper
- Glue or paste diluted with water
- A paintbrush
- Ribbons and bows

To do another project, she also gathers:

- Old paper bags or newspaper

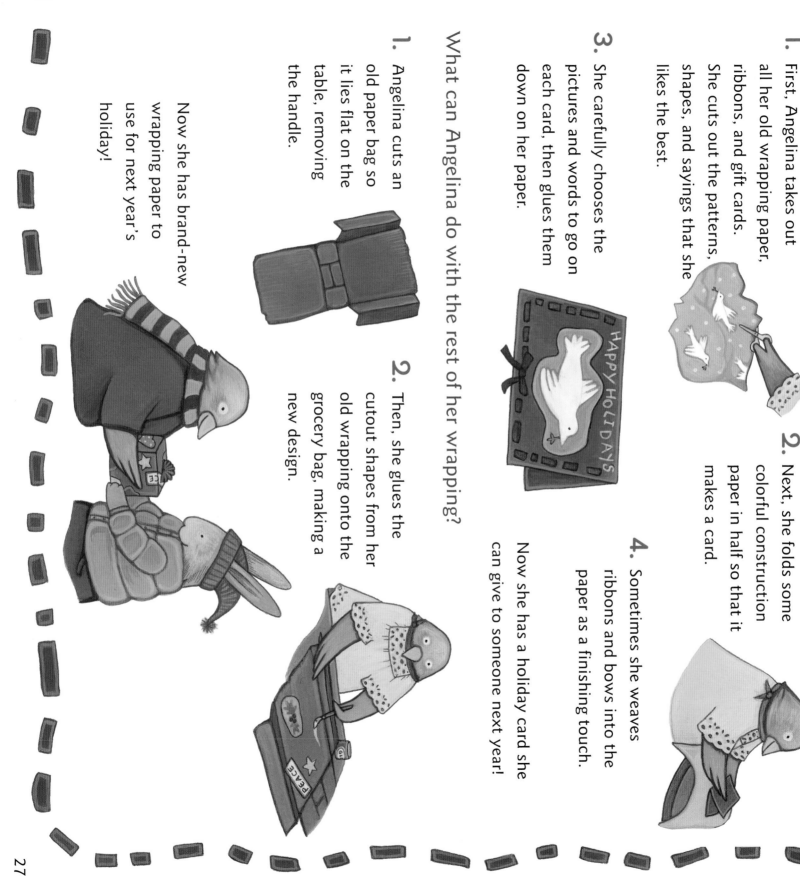

1. First, Angelina takes out all her old wrapping paper, ribbons, and gift cards. She cuts out the patterns, shapes, and sayings that she likes the best.

2. Next, she folds some colorful construction paper in half so that it makes a card.

3. She carefully chooses the pictures and words to go on each card, then glues them down on her paper.

4. Sometimes she weaves ribbons and bows into the paper as a finishing touch.

Now she has a holiday card she can give to someone next year!

What can Angelina do with the rest of her wrapping?

1. Angelina cuts an old paper bag so it lies flat on the table, removing the handle.

2. Then, she glues the cutout shapes from her old wrapping onto the grocery bag, making a new design.

Now she has brand-new wrapping paper to use for next year's holiday!

Andrew's toys are taking over his room—
there's no space to read or to play.
Building blocks sit where his pillow should be,
and three bicycles get in the way.

A legion of LEGOs has captured his dresser—
they're building themselves up the wall.
The puzzles composed of thousands of pieces
are creeping out into the hall. . . .

What can you do with too many toys?

Andrew gathers:

- All the toys, games, and books
  he doesn't use
- A phone book
- A grown-up

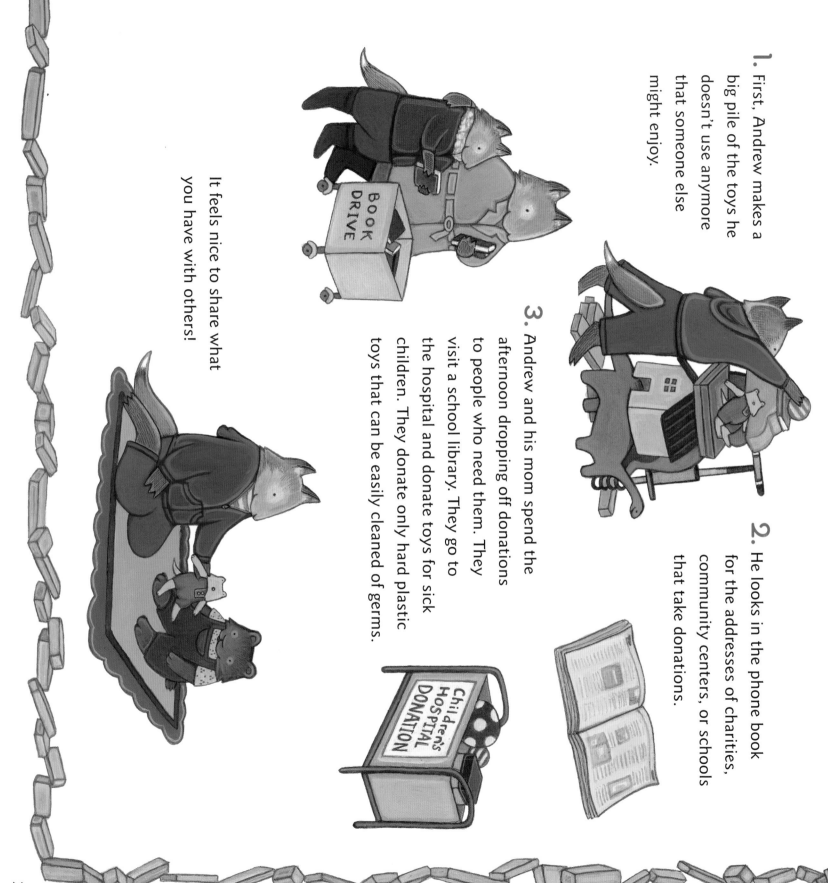

1. First, Andrew makes a big pile of the toys he doesn't use anymore that someone else might enjoy.

2. He looks in the phone book for the addresses of charities, community centers, or schools that take donations.

3. Andrew and his mom spend the afternoon dropping off donations to people who need them. They visit a school library. They go to the hospital and donate toys for sick children. They donate only hard plastic toys that can be easily cleaned of germs.

It feels nice to share what you have with others!

What else can you do to support reuse and recycling?

Tips for Kids and Grown-ups

KIDS

- When you make a drawing, use both sides of the piece of paper, instead of two separate sheets.

- Use a lunchbox instead of a paper bag to carry your lunch to school.

- After you use a plastic bag, rinse it out and let it dry so that you can use it again.

- Before discarding an old plastic or glass food container, wash it out and use it for another purpose, such as storing art or school supplies.

- Save Styrofoam food trays and wash them thoroughly. When they dry, use them as paint palettes, a surface to draw on, or turn them into stamps.

- When you go to the park, bring a plastic bag to collect any recyclable trash you find (tin cans, plastic bottles, cardboard boxes, etc.). Work with an adult to determine which items are okay to pick up, bring home, and recycle.

- Write to companies that make products with packaging that is not recyclable and ask them to change how they package their products so that they can help the environment, too.

THE WHOLE FAMILY

- Buy recycled products, such as toilet paper, stationery, and computer supplies.

- Avoid buying items that come in packaging that's not recyclable.

- Take a cloth bag with you when you go shopping so you won't need plastic or paper bags.

- If you have extra plastic bags, use them as liners in your trash cans.

- Replace disposable products around the house with reusable items. For instance, replace paper napkins with cloth, paper towels with dish towels, and paper and plastic plates with reusable dishes.

- Use plastic or glass bottles to store drinks for kids' lunches instead of juice boxes. Also, get reusable storage containers to hold the food in their lunchbox, rather than using plastic bags or aluminum foil.

- When you go to a restaurant, bring a reusable plastic or glass container to take home your leftovers.

- Donate your old computer equipment to a school, or contact a computer recycling center so that it can be used for parts.

- Donate your old cell phone for reuse; facilities can be found online. Cell phones can also be brought to stores to be recycled for parts or given to classrooms for their playhouse areas.

- Start a recycling program at your local school or community center.

Hand-sewing tips

BACK SIDE

How do you sew a "whipstitch" like Ben?

1. Starting in a corner, push a threaded needle up through both pieces of fabric that you are sewing together.

2. Bring the needle over the edges of the fabric and back to the side where you first inserted the needle.

3. Push the needle up through both pieces of fabric again, a short distance from where you started. This will create a diagonal line. Pull firmly.

4. Repeat this action, creating diagonal lines over the edges of your fabric.

How do you sew a "running stitch" like Jack?

1. Starting in a corner, push a threaded needle up through both pieces of fabric that you are sewing together.

2. Push your needle back down again through both pieces of fabric a short distance from where you began.

3. Repeat this action in a straight line, keeping the size of the stitches small and even. The length of the stitches should be about as long as the spaces between them.

Note: If you have trouble sewing in a straight line, try drawing a line on your fabric with a pencil, then sew along the line you have drawn.

What do you do when you've finished your stitching?

1. Sew three little stitches in place, on top of each other, at the end of your seam.

2. Pull the thread tight.

3. Cut the thread close to the stitches.